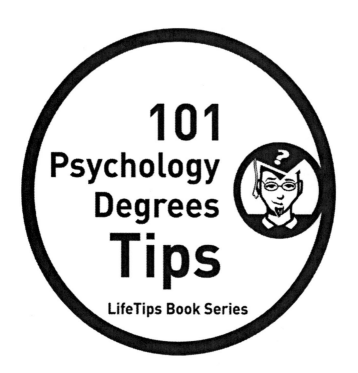

101
Psychology
Degrees
Tips

LifeTips Book Series

By Jolyn Wells-Moran, Ph.D.
Psychology Degree Guru
LifeTips

D1700849

LifeTips Book Series
Boston, Massachusetts

LIFETIPS PRESIDENT: Byron White
BOOK SERIES EDITOR: Melanie Nayer

LifeTips.com, Inc.
101 Book Series
One First Avenue
Building 34, Suite 200
Charlestown, MA 02129
(617) 886-9001
http://www.LifeTips.com

International Standard Book No. 978-1-60275-012-8

Table of Contents

No matter what you choose to study or which career path you follow, success is a struggle. As part of our educational tips series, Jolyn Wells-Moran, Ph.D., examines the various aspects of psychology degrees, how to choose a psychology degree program and what it takes to succeed in the psychology field.

This tip book also examines in detail the various types of psychology degrees offered at some of the finest universities. From behavioral and cognitive to humanistic and neuropsychology, potential psychology students can get a full overview of the courses, timelines and career opportunities available in their selected field.

Dr. Joyce Brothers, American psychologist, TV-radio personality, columnist and author put it perfectly when she said, "Success is a state of mind. If you want success, start thinking of yourself as a success."

Melanie Nayer
LifeTips Editor

A Note from the Author

Everyone has psychological theories, but people who really want to know what the great minds have theorized and truths about psychology seek an education in it. To those who pursue it, psychology is an intriguing field; challenging throughout a lifetime, frequently surprising, and with varied education and career opportunities. This book is meant to provide the information necessary for readers at any stage of education to make wise choices about the match between their psychology interests, and their psychology education and career goals. Whether an individual is seeking a future career in the field or not, though, the foundation that a psychology education provides can always be useful to that person's career, personal growth, formation of positive relationships and creation of a meaningful life.

Psychology is such a complex topic. There are thousands of concepts, theories and research findings concerning it, and there are just as many applications for it. As a result, finding out what types of psychology there are, the kinds of degrees available, and how these fit in with your psychology or other career aspirations can be hopelessly difficult. This book will answer many of the questions you have now, if you're interested in attaining a psychology degree, and also questions you haven't thought to ask yet. It will also lead you to sources that can help you further in your quest for an education in psychology.

Jolyn Wells-Moran, Ph.D.
LifeTips Expert Guru

1| Choosing Your Psychology College

Where you go to school for your first Psychology Degree will probably depend on several factors. Where you go to school for a graduate or doctoral degree will matter more, though. You may decide to get an Associate's Degree and go to a community college for it, or go to a community college before going on to a four-year college or university for a Bachelor's Degree. You can also choose to go into a four-year college or university without attending a community college if you meet the admissions criteria. There may be some potential pros and cons of attending a community college first and we'll discuss some of those in the next section.

You may choose a private or state college or university. At this beginning level, and if you plan to or think you might continue on with your psychology education, you needn't consider whether the courses fit exactly what you think you'll need for your career. However, you might need to look at; financial aid options, your costs, campus housing, location, the range and types of Psychology courses offered, the quality and reputation of the school if you think you might want to continue on into graduate school, classroom sizes, availability and quality of instructors, internship opportunities, job placement services, the size of the school, whether you can meet the admissions criteria and other considerations. These may all be important variables in choosing a graduate school or doctoral program too, but by the time you're ready for either, you'll know more clearly what you want to do in the field, where and with whom. At these levels, you'll have more of such choices to make from more specific options.

2| Community Colleges

Community colleges often offer several benefits over other colleges and universities, but there may be some downside points as well. Weigh both sides before you decide for or against attending a community college. Many students complete one or two years at a community college before transferring to a four-year college or university. Community colleges cost less, can usually accept students with a broader range of GPAs and test scores, are often easier to get into than some colleges and many universities, and usually have smaller class sizes. They're also often in areas that have no other colleges or universities nearby and generally employ high quality, committed instructors. They often offer courses during evenings and even weekends since many community college students also have jobs. On the more negative side, community colleges often have no student housing and comparatively lackluster student activities on campus. They may have a higher percentage of students who aren't particularly inclined towards academia than other colleges, and this can be difficult for more academically oriented students. The workload for many community college courses tends to be less rigorous too.

3| Finding a College

There are a few good ways to learn about colleges where you can earn a Psychology Degree. If you're in high school, see your counseling office for their information on colleges. If you're out of high school, you can visit a college campus and see the catalogs in their counseling office. Seeing a counselor is always a good idea. They know many resources, frequently have software and may be members of web sites with information that can help. Some counselors also know some specific information that you can't find easily in print.

➜

4| Private Colleges

Private colleges and universities sometimes have significant private sources of financial aid for students and excellent faculty. Classes are sometimes smaller than at larger state institutions too. They are frequently costly since they are not subsidized with government funding. Some are among the most prestigious schools of higher education. However, not all private colleges and universities are the same, just as there are many differences between state funded colleges and universities. Some people choose private, church affiliated schools. Others may choose a private school because of location or because a parent or grandparent attended it. Still others may be drawn by the quality of education and curricular choices of certain private school. You may find some other benefits or drawbacks as you explore the possibilities.

5| State Colleges and Universities

State colleges and universities are subsidized by their states, so the costs of attendance are lower for state residents than at private colleges and universities. Many state colleges and universities have excellent reputations for academic excellence, vibrant student life, and a range of programs or departments and courses. Housing is often available on or near campus. The costs can be high for tuition for students who are not state residents, although scholarships, grants and/or loans may be available. In the undergraduate years, in particular, class sizes may be very large, in the hundreds in large lecture halls, and it may be very difficult to arrange one-on-one time with instructors. If you're considering research, you may want to find out about research projects on campus with which you might be able to become involved. Be sure to look carefully at the course catalog and requirements for graduation.

6| How to Choose Your Psychology Discipline

It's always a good idea to check with a career counselor when you want to know if you should choose a specific discipline and need help sorting through all of the possible variables involved in making a choice. If you find it makes sense to choose a specific psychology discipline, you'll most likely decide this and have opportunity to do so when you're looking at master's and doctoral programs. There are relatively few simple choices of careers paths in psychology, though.

Some psychology disciplines are well suited to the job market and others aren't. Some types of psychology are best used in specific settings, such as Human Factors Psychology which is used in industrial settings. Some psychologies are best suited to particular populations. Job markets vary between regions, states, cities and rural areas too. These are just a few of the factors a counselor can help you include in your decision-making.

7| When to Choose Your Psychology Discipline

There isn't a great need, or usually much opportunity, to concentrate in one specific area of Psychology before graduate school (master's degree level). Think of your psychology education as a career path that will unfold as you explore more about it in college and while working in the field. You'll know much more about psychology, its applications and how you want to apply your education by the time you're ready for a master's program. You may instead want or need to work in the field before you continue for a higher Degree in Psychology. This can be another way to discover more about potential opportunities in the field and your own preferences. You may also decide that an Associate's or Bachelor's Degree in Psychology is as far as you want to go in school, or that you'd rather continue on in a related or different field. Psychology is an excellent foundation, as mentioned earlier in this book, for other studies and careers. Still another scenario might be that you have a bachelor's degree in something other than Psychology and decide to go into a Master's in Psychology program. If and when you get to the point of looking at Master's programs in Psychology, there are choices of more discipline-oriented programs or more eclectic ones. The same is true if you already have a Master's Degree in Psychology and are looking at doctoral programs. In any case, a somewhat broad-based education in Psychology may provide a broader range of job opportunities than you would have otherwise. These are choices to discuss with a college advisor.

→

8| Admissions: Getting up to Speed

You may need to take some remedial courses and these are often available at community colleges. You may also elect to attend a community college for an Associate's Degree for the purpose of going on into a four-year program, or as preparation for qualifying for work that requires an Associate's Degree. Talk to college personnel where you've applied or would like to apply to find out what you can do to qualify for the program you want to enter there.

➡

9| Admissions and Costs

Your GPA and the costs of college will be only two of the factors for your consideration in choosing and being admitted to a college. You must have graduated from high school or have earned a high school equivalency. Colleges also consider college admissions test (SAT, ACT or another one) scores. Your extracurricular activities and, perhaps, participation in outside activities such as employment, volunteer work and community organizations may count too.

If your GPA is below the required one and the average GPA of people admitted to the college, you may decide to forego applying there. If it's close, then you should look at the number of people admitted in the last couple of years and the number who applied. If the competition has been high, as is true of many high prestige schools and large universities, then you may not have much of a chance. Add in your extracurricular, other activities and test score(s). If these aren't particularly impressive, your application is probably a long shot.

If your main concern is financial aid and not whether you can get into the college, talk with your high school counseling office or the college's financial aid office. Never assume that you won't be able to attend a college of your choice if you qualify, just because you can't afford it. Scholarships come in more than merit- and need-based forms. Some depend on a family member's membership in the sponsoring organization or other factors.

Your GPA and the costs of college will be only two of the factors for your consideration in choosing and being admitted to a college. You must have graduated from high school or have earned a high school equivalency. Colleges also consider college admissions test (SAT, ACT or another one) scores. Your extracurricular activities and, perhaps, participation in outside activities such as employment, volunteer work and community organizations may count too.

If your GPA is below the required one and the average GPA of people admitted to the college, you may decide to forego applying there. If it's close, then you should look at the number of people admitted in the last couple of years and the number who applied. If the competition has been high, as is true of many high prestige schools and large universities, then you may not have much of a chance. Add in your extracurricular, other activities and test score(s). If these aren't particularly impressive, your application is probably a long shot.

If your main concern is financial aid and not whether you can get into the college, talk with your high school counseling office or the college's financial aid office. Never assume that you won't be able to attend a college of your choice if you qualify, just because you can't afford it. Scholarships come in more than merit- and need-based forms. Some depend on a family member's membership in the sponsoring organization or other factors.

10| Admissions: Test Results

You might want to take the SAT, ACT, GRE or other required test again if you didn't do well, Study for the sections where you didn't do as well as you think you could. If you were distracted, ill or made strategic test-taking errors, you may be able to improve your score. You can also talk to someone in admissions to find out if taking any kind of college courses first, perhaps at a community college, can help you with admissions later. The college may also consider placing you in a probationary status, with continuance as a student there dependent on your earning credits in a course elsewhere or achieving a certain GPA in college. You may want to take the college admissions test again if your scores are an issue as they stand.

11| The Essay or Letter

Find out as exactly as possible what the school is looking for in the application letter or essay. Make sure you meet the deadline. Use your best written English, make the letter or essay as clear as you can, include complete answers to questions and/or the description of what they're looking for, have it proofed by one or more other people who have strong written English skills. Finally, make the corrections and submit clean, white pages with standard margins using a 12-point Ariel, Helvetica or Times font in black ink: Otherwise, if the school has provided instructions for the margins and font, follow those.

12| How to Pay for College

See the financial aid office on campus or, if you're in high school, talk to an advisor. There are also many web sites, books and other printed materials that can provide you with financial advice concerning payment of costs of college. Scholarships, loans and grants are available to many, if not most, prospective students and current college students.

Don't let cost deter you from higher education, but do be reasonable about choosing a college you can afford if it means you don't qualify for scholarships or grants. Think carefully, too, about whether to take out any student loans. Make sure that you're being realistic about what you'll be able to afford to pay back after you graduate. If the job market projections are good, you know you won't have other substantial obligations for the period of the loan and your field pays well, then taking out a college loan may be a relatively safe thing way to pay for some college costs.

Be sure to figure in the costs of housing, food, books and other materials, transportation, tuition, college fees, parking, car insurance spending money and anything else. Now is a good time to simplify and contain your costs too, perhaps by foregoing use of a car and reducing the amount of spending money you'll need. You may also want to consider part-time college attendance, giving you opportunity for more work hours while in college and reducing your college costs.

13| What Is An Associate's Degree?

An Associate's Degree is considered an undergraduate degree. Some of the courses required are not directly related to Psychology, but are useful to success in Psychology courses and to gaining a higher degree later on. Those courses, such as English, often help students learn skills that are helpful within a job too. Most colleges require further English, Science and Math courses beyond high school levels, in addition to Psychology courses. Some of the psychological theories and concepts may seem strange at first, but most students who stick with it find that the content becomes more clear. Many students also feel frustrated with these foundation courses because it's difficult to see how they will ever be able to apply the knowledge. Again, in time and with further study, most students find that the knowledge they've gained is applicable to whatever work they do with people. An Associate's Degree is usually considered a paraprofessional degree. You might be able to work serving people as an aide or in another entry level position within a mental health, developmental disabilities or another human service organization with an AA or an AS. With an Associate's Degree, you would probably be supervised by someone with a higher degree or more experience.

14| AA in Psychology

An AA in Psychology is an Associate in Arts Degree with a major in Psychology. Students working towards an AA in Psychology must usually take the basic courses required for any Associate's Degree, such as one or more English courses and perhaps one or more Science, Math, History or Foreign Language courses. They are also required to complete certain Humanities and Psychology courses, some of which may be taken as electives.

15| Building From Your Associate's Degree

An Associate's Degree in Science (AS) will transfer best to a Bachelor's Degree in Science (BS). If you later prefer to earn a BA, rather than a BS, you will probably be required to take some additional courses.

16| Accredited Online Associate's Degree in Psychology

An Associate's Degree in Psychology may also be earned through an accredited online education program, some of which are through colleges and universities.

The other questions to answer:

· Is the program offered through a known community college, four-year college, university or well-recognized online education institution? (If it is, that's some assurance that the quality of the program will be good.)

· What are the faculty qualifications listed on the web site or in materials you order from the web site or by phone? (Look for at least Master's level educated instructors, where their degrees were earned and years of teaching experience. You might also want to see if any of the faculty specialize, or have experience in, a particular aspect of Psychology that interests you.)

· Does the curriculum look similar to other programs' curricula and make sense to you?

· Does the program require a high school degree or equivalency? (Credible Associate degree programs require a high school degree or equivalency, unless it's a special program designed for earning the high school equivalency or otherwise gaining the knowledge and skills of high school equivalency while completing the Associate program.)

· Is there a trial version of a course on the web site so that you can test the ease of online participation or are you already familiar with the program they use for online participation? (If you aren't familiar with it, then test the trial version. If there is no trial version, email or call them and ask for a trial version.)

· Is the cost of the program comparable to other programs you're considering, and if not, does the quality appear to be less or better than those of of other programs enough to justify the cost difference? (You might also want to think about how credible your degree will look on your resume if it's from one institution as compared to another.)

Some colleges and universities offer a combination, or choices, of on-campus and online courses that can be applied towards an Associate Degree in Psychology. There are pros and cons to taking both online and on-campus courses. These include the possible rewards and enhanced learning through development of strong relationships with faculty and other students when taking courses on campus, and the convenience of not having to appear on campus for classes when taking courses online.

17| How Long Does It Take to Complete An Associate's Degree?

An Associate's Degree usually requires four semesters or six quarters of full-time study; approximately two school years. Programs vary in how long they allow a part-time student to earn the degree. An Associate's Degree in Psychology may be earned at a community college, four- year college or university, depending on the institution. Some colleges and universities offer Psychology Degree programs and some don't.

→

18| BA vs. BS in Psychology

It depends on what higher degree program you choose. A Bachelor's in Arts Degree in Psychology can be applied towards a Master's of Arts Degree in Psychology, and also to some other related Arts Degree programs. A BA in Psychology is most likely to transfer without taking any or many further courses before admission to a Master's in Arts Degree in Psychology, or maybe a Master's in Psychology (MPsy) program. Other courses will probably be required before admission to a Masters in Arts program in a related or different field. Applying a BA in Psychology towards an MS in Psychology or another sciences program would require, most likely and at least, more science coursework.

19| Obtaining a Bachelor's Degree in Psychology

An Associate's Degree may be a first step towards a Bachelor's Degree in Psychology or a Bachelor's Degree in another subject if you choose to continue your higher education. A Bachelor's Degree usually takes about two more school years of fulltime study, but may take somewhat longer. A Master's Degree can be earned after a Bachelor's Degree, and after the Master's, a Doctorate.

20| Bachelor of Science in Psychology

A BS in Psychology is a Bachelor's in Sciences Degree with a major in Psychology. For a BS, emphasis is generally on General Education and the Sciences, in addition to Psychology. There are many human service jobs that require a BS, or a BA, in Psychology or a related field. The BS in Psychology is considered a paraprofessional degree. Yet, there are some professional positions filled by people with BS in Psychology Degrees. For example, you may choose to work in a setting where the BS, or a BA, is the highest degree required. There are also organizations where BS level personnel are supervised by people with masters or doctoral degrees. In the latter, there are often pay, role and autonomy differences in the workplace between employees with undergraduate degrees -- like the AS, BS, AA and BA -- and graduate degrees. Since the BS requires greater emphasis on the sciences, it will better prepare you for an entry-level research job than will a BA. It also transfers more easily than a BA to a higher science degree. This doesn't mean you can't transfer to an arts degree to a higher degree in the sciences, but you would very likely need to take additional science courses before admission to a science program.

21| Undergraduate Degrees in Psychology

A BA, Bachelor's in Arts, and a BS, Bachelor's in Science, are both undergraduate degrees. Although a Bachelor's Degree is a step up from an Associate's Degree, both the Bachelor's and the Associate's are considered undergraduate, paraprofessional degrees. It usually takes about four school years, eight semesters or 12 quarters, of full-time enrollment to earn a Bachelor's. If an Associate's Degree was earned first, the Bachelor's usually takes about two more school years. Many schools allow part-time enrollment too. Community colleges, since they are two-year schools, do not usually offer upper division Bachelor's level courses unless a four-year college or university happens to offer them through the community college.

22| Teaching Psychology

An undergraduate degree in Psychology may be a step towards teaching Psychology or another subject. Teaching Psychology in a larger college or university usually requires at least a Master's or Doctorate in Psychology, such as an MA, MS, MPsy, MEd in Psychology, EdD, PsyS, PsyD or PhD in Psychology, just as teaching Math at the college level usually requires a Master's or Doctorate in Mathematics.

Teaching at a university or college may not require an actual teaching degree, depending on the institution and sometimes the state. Again, a Psychology undergraduate degree is considered one of up to several possible foundation degrees for other fields.

Teaching children in a public school, and often in a private one, requires an undergraduate or graduate teaching -- otherwise referred to as a Degree in Education degree. In this case, the BA or BS in Psychology would need to be followed by, at least, either by a Bachelor's of Arts Degree in Education (BA), usually with a teaching certificate to follow, or a Master's Degree in Education (MEd), also often with a teaching certificate. A Master's is a more competitive degree than a BA or BS in the K – 12 teaching arena.

A required teaching certificate, and even the course content for the certificate, is often state mandated. Earning the certificate may require up to several more months of education and, often, an internship in teaching. Private schools are less often regulated by states and so hire without a teaching certificate. Someone with a Bachelor's in Psychology may also be able to take some education and perhaps other courses, and then earn the teaching certificate. Check your state education regulations.

Teaching in a community, or sometimes in another small college setting, usually requires a graduate degree, although a teaching degree of any sort may not be required. Vocational and technical schools differ widely in their requirements of teachers.

23| Completing Your Bachelor's Degree in Psychology

Most courses you take for an AA or AS will transfer towards a Bachelor's Degree. Whether you choose a Bachelor's Degree in Arts (BA) or a Bachelor's Degree in Science (BS) should depend on three primary factors: 1) your career goals; 2) whether you're more oriented towards the arts or the sciences; and 3) any plan you may have for a certain Master's or Doctoral Degree. If you've already earned an AA or AS and then want to change from Arts to Sciences, or Sciences to Arts, for your Bachelor's, you may need to consider the time and effort you'll need to invest in taking extra courses before and after acceptance into your preferred BA or BS program. In the long run, though, a few extra courses should never mean the difference between choosing your ideal education and career goals or not. What may seem like a frustrating delay to you now is likely to seem inconsequential in hindsight, especially after you've taken dozens of more courses for your Bachelor's and/or Master's Degrees. Remember that the point of education is really to gain as much knowledge and as many skills as you can.

24| A Master's in Psychology

In the US, a Master's in Psychology usually refers to either a Master's in Arts (MA) or Master's in Sciences (MS) Degree with a major in Psychology, while an MPsy may refer to a Master's in Metaphysical Psychology. Some other countries, such as the UK and Australia, offer what is called a Master's in Psychology, or MPsy. Their MPsy programs are only very generally like Master's in Psychology programs in the US, have different admissions requirements and often take four years to earn .

25| Finding Psychology Graduate Schools

Each December the American Psychologist journal publishes a list of accredited psychology graduate schools. Students interested in pursuing advanced degrees in psychology can use this list to determine whether or not a school they are considering is accredited. This information can also be found online at the American Psychological Association (APA) website. On this website students can not only view a list of accredited psychology schools but will also find information on schools which were denied accreditation and schools which were previously accredited but no longer hold this distinction.

This information is extremely useful to students considering psychology graduate schools as schools which are accredited will be most beneficial to the student pursuing career options as well as additional degrees. Students may also learn a great deal about psychology graduate schools through the career counseling office of their undergraduate school.

These career counselors likely have a great deal of up to date information about the available options for students and likely are contacted by the schools periodically with updates about the school and the programs offered to ensure the counselors can provide the students with accurate information.

Related Tip: There is a great deal of information online in regard to psychology graduate schools. Students may opt to visit the website of a particular graduate school to learn more about the school or may visit websites which compile information on a number of different psychology graduate schools. However, before making a final decision about which school to attend, the student should verify the schools accreditation either through the December issue of the American Psychologist journal or through the American Psychological Association website.

→

26| The Master's in Arts (MA) in Psychology

A Master's in Arts (MA) in Psychology is a Master's Degree in Arts with a major in Psychology. This is considered a professional level degree and usually takes one or two full-time school years to complete; two to four semesters or three to six quarters, depending on the program. A prior Bachelor's Degree is normally required as a prerequisite to a Master's Degree program. If the Bachelor's Degree wasn't in Psychology, then at least certain courses in Psychology are required for admission to a Psychology Masters program.

27| The Master's in Science (MS) in Psychology

A Master's in Sciences (MS) in Psychology is a Master's Degree in Sciences with a major in Psychology. This is also considered a professional level degree and usually takes one or two full-time school years to complete; two to four semesters or three to six quarters, depending on the program. Again, a Bachelor's Degree is normally required as a prerequisite to a Master's Degree program. If the Bachelor's Degree wasn't in Psychology, then at least certain courses in Psychology are required before admission to a Psychology Masters program.

28| The Master's in Education (MEd) in Educational Psychology

The term, Master's in Education Psychology, refers to a Master's in Education (MEd) with a concentration in Educational Psychology. Some people use the longer form after their names. MEd, EdPsy, or in conversation may say they have a MEd in Educational Psychology. There is not a degree specifically called a Master's in Education or Educational Psychology. The M.Ed. in Psychology may be somewhat similar to a Master's in Psychology (MS and MA), but the emphasis will be on psychology as applied to education, such as special education, K-12 education, higher education, education administration or another aspect of education.

29| MS to Doctoral Degree in Psychology

It's sometimes not necessary to earn a Master's Degree before you'll be admitted to a Psychology Doctorate program. In fact, in some doctoral programs you may have to repeat some of the coursework you took in a master's program. This depends on the program. You may otherwise be able to waive some of the repeated courses in the doctoral program, again depending on the program. If you think want to work in the field before going on for a Doctorate, though, or aren't absolutely sure you'll go into a doctoral program at all, then earning your Master's in Psychology first has some advantages. You'll likely earn more and be qualified for a more responsible and autonomous position with a Master's Degree.

30| Working Toward the Master of Science in Psychology

A BS in Psychology may be a step towards an MS in Psychology, a Master's in Psychology or another type of Master's in Science degree. The foundations in the sciences you've gained by earning a BS will prepare you best for another sciences degree. Most, if not all, of your undergraduate sciences credits will count towards admission into a graduate sciences program in Psychology. This doesn't mean you could choose only a higher degree in a science, but if you choose to apply to an arts program instead, you would probably be required to complete more humanities courses before admission and maybe even more Psychology.

Don't let this keep you from choosing a BS, though, since this would likely only be a delay of months if you later decide to go on for a Master in Arts majoring in Psychology. A lot depends on what you hope to do with your degree, whether you are oriented or not towards the sciences and your capabilities and competencies in the sciences and arts. You may decide to earn a BS because you want the foundation science courses for later graduate science study. You might decide on the BS because it would give you enough science foundation for work you want to do in the field, with or without a graduate degree in a science. You may also choose a BS, or a BA, degree to help you decide whether to choose a graduate sciences or arts degree.

31| Doctorates in Psychology

There are two types of doctoral degrees in psychology, a PhD and a PsyD. There are other related doctoral options too, depending on your career goals. These include doctorates in allied fields, such as the EdD (Doctor of Education), Ph.D. in Social Work (Doctor of Philosophy in Social Work) and Psychiatry and nursing with a specialization in serving people with mental illnesses. If you are interested in psychiatry, you'll need a medical doctorate. If you're interested in Psychiatric Nursing, you'll need some level of nursing degree.

32| The Psy.D.

PsyD means Doctor of Psychology. This degree also generally takes four to seven years to complete. There is less of a science focus in PsyD programs than in PhD programs and more training in direct practice, although there is some science in PsyD programs too. PsyD programs claim to prepare graduates for a wider array of settings, although there is little difference in getting jobs between the two. One exception may be in qualifying to teach Psychology at the college level, where a PhD is generally better recognized.

33| The EdD in Psychology

The EdD (Doctor of Education) in Psychology and the PhD in Educational Psychology are closely allied to the psychology doctorates, but tend to focus on research and applications of psychology in education settings. The focus may be on special education, k-12, higher education or education administration.

34| The PhD in Psychology

A PhD in Psychology is a Doctor of Philosophy majoring in, for instance, Clinical Psychology. Otherwise, the PhD may be in Counseling or Research Psychology. It takes between four and seven years to complete such a doctoral program. The scientific model, often called empirical research, and academic scholarship are more emphasized than in PsyD programs. An individual with a Ph D in Clinical Psychology and another with a PsyD often hold the same types of positions in the workforce, including consultation, policy-making, administrative, private practice, college level teaching, psychological testing, counseling/therapy and others. The PhD is more widely accepted as a teaching degree at some universities than is the PsyD. The PhD in Clinical Psychology is geared more towards helping people with mental illnesses, as opposed to Counseling Psychology which tends to emphasize working with people on life issues. The PhD in Research Psychology often best qualifies the individual for research, academic and psychological testing positions. The PhD in Counseling Psychology tends to prepare people for private practice, or counseling, as the name implies, but also for testing and other positions. It may be helpful to remember that Counseling Psychology evolved from guidance and career counseling when recalling the difference between it and Clinical Psychology.

35| The PhD in Social Work

The PhD in Social Work is somewhat similar to the PhD in Psychology and the PsyD. However, it draws from various areas of Psychology, Sociology and a body of knowledge of it's own. It has it's own code of ethics and professional associations. Social Work is particularly geared towards disadvantaged groups. When assessing individuals and groups, it claims to be more likely to consider the effects of the environment on the person, as well as the person's individual psychology and Sociology's group behavior. This is a broad generalization, as there are various disciplines within Social Work, just as in Psychology. A degree in Psychiatry is also similar in some respects to a Doctorate in Psychology. The two are frequently confused with each other, but a Psychiatrist has a medical degree. Both may see patients in therapy or counseling, although a Psychiatrist can prescribe medications: A Psychologist cannot prescribe medications, except currently in one state. Likewise, there are nursing degrees with a specialization in serving people who have mental illnesses, known as Psychiatric Nursing.

36| Behavioral Psychology

Behavioral Psychology is grounded in empirical research. The rational approach -- observable behavior in reaction to external stimuli -- is its focus. The effects of rewards, punishments, and association on learning have been studied extensively by Behavioral Psychologists (or Behaviorists). Early work includes the example of Pavolv's Dog, the dog that salivated when a bell rang because he had been conditioned to associate the ring with food. Watson and Skinner are other famous names from Behavioral Psychology.

37| Rationalism in Behavioral Psychology

Rationalism, as applied within Behavioral Psychology, contends that understanding of human behavior is best approached by the application of logic. Logical reasoning requires observable and quantifiable science, often referred to as empiricism. This is quite different from qualitative study of research that, for instances, may rely on case studies or even what we often refer to as common sense.

38| Behavioral Psychology's Achievements and Criticisms

Behavioral Psychology, or Behaviorism, is often both applauded and criticized for its emphasis on rationalism and mechanism. Those who believe Psychology can always, or almost always, be explained as conditioned behavior are drawn to Behavioral Psychology. Some people choose it because it reasonably accounts for certain psychological problems they're interested in exploring further, such as dangerous behaviors. Others choose it because they are drawn to the empirical science of it, or are particularly adept in science. Behavioral Psychology has been shown to be an important component of some types of learning, although not all. It has been used successfully for certain purposes, as in intensive behavioral interventions. Criticisms of Behavioral Psychology, or behaviorism in general, often contend that human Psychology is too complex to take only an empirical and/or behavioral approach to it. Critiques include the views that human beings are; not as mechanistic, or like machines, as behaviorism suggests; able to change even their reinforced learning as may be needed or desired; and can learn in other ways too.

39| Cognitive-Behavioral Therapy

Cognitive-behavioral therapy is an important derivative of Behavioral Psychology, otherwise called CBT. It combines cognitive theories and approaches with behavioral theories and approaches within the therapeutic setting. There are several types of CBT, but the common thread is the belief that our cognition (thinking) leads to our emotions and behaviors. This is a popular therapeutic approach that teaches individuals to change problem behaviors or emotions by learning to think different thoughts and/or to think in different ways to achieve different feelings and/or behaviors.

40| Mechanism in Behavioral Psychology

Mechanism, within Behavioral Psychology, is a view of human behavior as being machine-like. The scope of mechanism within Behavioral Psychology ranges from some to what can be called a radical degree. It is not necessary to discount other psychologies in favor of behaviorism in academic study or practice: In fact, most psychologists have a working knowledge of behavioral theory and approaches, even if they claim to be eclectic practitioners or their primary approach is something quite different.

41| Cognitive Psychology

Cognitive (and/or Perceptual) Psychology looks at mental processes, such as memory, problem-solving, reflection, decision-making, perception and other aspects of how human beings think. In therapy, a Cognitive Psychologist, or another professional trained in Cognitive Psychology may, as examples, want to help an individual learn better problem-solving skills or challenge distorted perceptions. Cognitive psychology has only been considered a branch of psychology since the late nineteen-sixties. Its theories have become common within other branches of psychology too. Many psychotherapies and education approaches incorporate theories of cognition now.

42| Cognitive Psychology and Computers

Remember the term "user-friendly"? It's important for designers in the computer and software design arenas to understand how people most often think about how to search or otherwise use computers and computer programs. They need to know what makes logical and/or intuitive sense when using computers, particularly to a majority of users. As examples, understanding something about sensory perceptions, memory, problem-solving and decision-making -- all aspects of Cognitive Psychology -- is critical.

43| The Study of Cognitive Psychology

Students of Cognitive Psychology are likely to study aspects of linguistics, logic, philosophy, behavioral psychology, human factors psychology, biological or neurological psychology, developmental psychology and related topics. Cognitive Psychology includes a complex set of inter-related, and sometimes, opposing theory. There are also several other types of cognitive therapy that are based on Cognitive Psychology, besides cognitive-behavioral therapy (CBT).

44| Cognitive-Behavioral Therapy (CBT)

Cognitive-Behavioral Therapy (CBT) is a vastly popular practical derivative of Cognitive Psychology that has shown success helping people with trauma, depression and personality disorders, to name a few applications. CBT relies on the recognition that our thoughts lead to our emotions and behaviors, and so to decrease distress or problem behaviors, the thoughts that lead to these need to be changed.

45| Cognitive Psychology Education

Cognitive Psychology is often paired with another discipline, or related discipline or terms, within higher education settings. Examples are; Neuropsychology/Cognitive Psychology, Behavioral/Cognitive Psychology, Communication/Cognitive Psychology and Perceptual/Cognitive Psychology. These programs are usually found at the graduate and doctoral levels, although there are often *courses* offered by the titles of Cognitive Psychology, Behavioral/Cognitive Psychology and others at the undergraduate level. Many undergraduate programs include the foundations, or at least aspects, of Cognitive Psychology as either courses or as part of other courses. Computer program design courses often include aspects of Cognitive Psychology too, as do many education courses.

46| Introduction to Developmental Psychology

Developmental Psychology is the study of human development from birth through old age. It's sometimes called, "Life-Span Psychology." There are many theories and concepts within Developmental Psychology, including Erik Erikson's famous paradigm of psychological tasks to be completed in order to achieve age-appropriate psychological maturity and personal success. Developmental Psychology is used in education, aging, therapy, child and family services, and other fields.

47| The Roots of Developmental Psychology

The history of modern developmental theories goes back to DesCartes, Rousseau, Locke and Darwin. Later, Freud's theory of psycho-sexual development is an example of what we now call Developmental Psychology. Jean Piaget's cognitive development model, Kohlberg's theory of moral development and many more theories and models followed. Discussion of norms, or normative human maturational stages are central to Developmental Psychology.

48| Applications of Developmental Psychology

There are many approaches to marriage and family counseling, substance abuse treatment, career counseling and several other populations, purposes and settings that are based on Developmental Psychology. It's a psychology rich in the kinds of research possibilities available too, and perhaps more than any other psychology, influences policy in education, social and other sectors as well. Developmental Psychology is often referenced in school and educational, organizational, personality, biological and other psychologies too. Explore more about Developmental Psychology to get a better sense of the many academic and career opportunities a knowledge of this psychology offers.

49| Exploring Developmental Psychology

There are no less than 1,650,000 pages using the keywords, Developmental Psychology, listed by Google. The Psi Cafe and the American Psychological Association's (APA) Developmental Psychology Links are good starting points. There are dozens of journals and many books on Developmental Psychology, too. You can also consult a career and academic counselor, an instructor of Developmental Psychology and people with degrees in Developmental Psychology to find out more about this broad category of psychology. Be aware that many Associate's, Bachelor's and Master's programs in Psychology offer courses in Developmental Psychology and you needn't major in Developmental Psychology to take some of them.

50| Evolutionary Psychology

Evolutionary Psychology refers to the distant biological heritage that still affects us cognitively, emotionally and behaviorally. It is more a term, rather than a distinct discipline within Psychology. Evolutionary Psychology may be used to explain such phenomena as the flight-or-flight response, as a popular example; a biological function inherited from our ancestors who sought to either fight with, or flee from, a saber-toothed tiger. As a Psychology, it is limited in scope since human thought, feelings and behaviors have likely become more complex over the eons. Yet, it is often considered to be an important aspect of understanding such questions as the nature of altruism, human aggression, gender roles and sexuality.

51| Practical Uses of Evolutionary Psychology

Evolutionary Psychology can help with understanding many areas of human behavior. Since it's also related to so many other psychologies and sciences, it can help with understanding those, too. As practical career examples, the study of aggression from an Evolutionary Psychology perspective would likely be of use by Forensic Psychologists and School Psychologists. The study of gender roles from an Evolutionary Psychology perspective might be of value in Feminist Psychology and Organizational Psychology practices. Another area of Evolutionary Psychology, the study of human sexuality, might be helpful in marriage and family, or couples, counseling. There may also be the opportunity of teaching Evolutionary Psychology courses, or including sections of it within certain courses, at the college level. There are many other applications as well.

52| Sciences Related to Evolutionary Psychology

Some colleges and universities offer Evolutionary Psychology courses and some offer Psychology Degrees majoring in Evolutionary Psychology. The degree may be paired with a related area, such as Evolutionary Psychology and Ethology (the study of animal behavior), Ecology or Cultural Anthropology (the study of human culture from ancient times to the present and how it has evolved). Evolutionary Psychology courses can often be taken as part of a Clinical, Research or Counseling Psychology Programs too. Some other sciences related to it that you might major in, and take some courses in Evolutionary Psychology for, also include; Sociology, Social Psychology, Biological Psychology, Neuropsychology and others.

53| Humanistic Psychology and Education

Although the height of the influence of Humanistic Psychology on education occurred during the 1970s with several educational experiments, such as open classrooms, other aspects of that impact remain in force. The ideas of curricular choice, learning opportunities concerning the arts, learning communities, and encouragement of creativity within the schools were borrowed from Humanistic Psychology. Perhaps most importantly, whether actually originated within Humanistic Psychology or expanded by it, the importance of the individual student is considered a focus of modern education.

54| Humanistic Psychology

Humanistic Psychology has been referred to as the *Third Force:* The *First Force* refers to behaviorism, a belief in conditioning as the predominant cause of human behavior, and to psychoanalytic psychology as the *Second Force,* the belief that the primary source of human behavior is the unconscious. Humanistic Psychology is a somewhat eclectic amalgam of constructivist, existential, phenomenological, transpersonal, feminist and other psychological theories and therapeutic approaches that are linked together by certain beliefs and values. Its pioneers included Fritz Perls, Carl Rogers and Abraham Maslow during the 1950s and 60s, although some of the roots go back to existentialism. The link between these theories and approaches is the central concern for what it is to be human. These tenets include, but are not limited to, the ideas that:

Life must be meaningful to the individual;

Human beings strive for wholeness;

Hope is necessary to life;

Creativity is an important, but higher order, phenomena;

The components of human psychological and physiological wellness;

The core of each person is good;

Each individual is unique;

There is a self to each person; and

That each human is always in a process of development.

Humanistic Psychology usually takes a qualitative approach to research, rather than a quantitative one. It was originally a psychology developed in reaction to what those in Humanistic Psychology saw as the mechanistic views of behaviorism and psychoanalysis. Humanistic Psychology is more apt to accept the subjective views of human beings about their experiences. It has had a far-reaching impact on our culture.

→

55| The Impact of Humanism

Psychotherapies under the heading of Humanistic Psychology include; the Feldenkreis Method, bioenergetics, encounter therapy, rational-emotive therapy, reality therapy and conjoint family therapy, among several others. Even Jungian Psychoanalysis is counted as a Humanistic Psychology, in spite of the fact that it is also referred to as belonging to psychoanalytic psychology. Yet, Humanistic Psychology, or humanism, has had a much broader impact than only in psychotherapies and human growth activities. Humanism has affected the burgeoning evolution of holistic health care, the feminist movement and other aspects of political and societal change since the 1960s. It is popularly credited with concern for self-esteem and the concepts of self-actualization, among many other popular ideas.

56| Self-Actualization

Self-Actualization is a widely used term that grew from Humanistic Psychology, and was coined by Abraham Maslow. He believed that once an individual's more basic needs are met, self-actualization is the natural goal towards which a person strives. The definition of self-actualization is reaching one's potential for maturity and mental health through exploration of the self and her or his environment. Self-actualization has had a significant impact on education.

57| Kinds of Psychology Degrees

There are choices of Clinical, Counseling and Research Psychology disciplines, but within these disciplines there are many kinds of Psychology. The kind you choose should depend on your interests, aspirations, capabilities and values. Your personal circumstances will ultimately determine whether you can afford the cost of the college or university program and want, or can, live where the institution is located. If you hope to work in the field, you should also consider the demand in the job market for the skills you'd gain. Once you've tentatively determined these, apply to a few programs in case you are turned down for your first choice.

58| Abnormal Psychology

Abnormal Psychology is the study of psychopathology, or behaviors and emotions that deviate from the norm. It looks at the disorders described in the DSM-IV TR, short for the Diagnostician's Statistical Manual that is widely used for diagnosis in North America. The DSM includes bipolar disorder, schizophrenia, borderline personality disorder and many other disorders.

59| Biological Psychology

Biological Psychology is based on quantifiable research of the brain and other physiological phenomena, including genetics that affect behavior, emotions and cognition. It's otherwise referred to as neuropsychology, behavioral neuroscience, biopsychology, psychobiology and physiological psychology. Biological Psychology uses fMRI (functional magnetic resonance imaging) and EEG (electroencephalography), among other tools, to diagnose physiological causes for psychopathology and other cognitive, behavioral and/or emotional states. It also draws from animal experimentation.

60| Clinical Psychology

Clinical Psychology includes theory, science and practice focused on the emotional states, psychological processes, interpersonal relations, cognitive functions and behaviors of human beings. Clinical Psychologists may work with any age in direct practice, or may work in research or administrative capacities.

61| Comparative Psychology

According to The American Psychological Association, the "focus of [Comparative Psychology] is on behavior and its relation to perception, learning, memory, cognition, motivation, and emotion" (2006). They refer to Comparative Psychologists as, "behavioral neuroscientists." If this seems confusing, especially after reading the Neuropsychology and Biological Psychology descriptions in this book, it is. Like those psychologies, Comparative Psychologists also study the brain and other physiological organs, systems and their functions. However, the difference is that Comparative Psychologists compare animal and human behaviors with particular attention to development and evolution.

62| Combining Psychology Degrees

As mentioned, there are many kinds of Psychology too, including; Sports, Abnormal, Biological, Forensic, School, Human Factors, Physiological, Art, Educational Psychology and more. Luckily, students don't have to choose a discipline until they've become familiar with what each kind entails. At the Associate's, Bachelor's and even somewhat at the Master's level in many programs, a cross-section of courses are required and offered. These provide students with an orientation to the kinds of Psychology from which they can choose and the chance to explore the kinds of Psychology they're interested in before making a commitment to one or two. As students progress to the Master's and Doctorate's levels in Psychology and choose the kind they'll major in, the focus narrows to provide more in-depth study. Only a person with a doctorate in Psychology is called a Psychologist.

63| Counseling Psychology

Counseling Psychology includes theory, science and practice focused on the emotions, psychology, social, cognitive and behavioral features of human beings. At times it appears that there isn't much difference between Clinical and Counseling Psychology, although Counseling Psychologists tend to work with people who are mentally stable, but have issues amenable to counseling or therapy while Clinical Psychologists study psychopathology and often work with people who have psychiatric disorders; also known as mental illnesses. Both Clinical and Counseling Psychologists who've earned degrees at the doctoral level can be licensed to practice as Psychologists and both are trained in psychotherapy. In many states, there is also licensing or certification with a Master's level degree in Psychology too, but the designation may be called something different, such as mental health specialist or therapist, and other people trained in other related disciplines may also qualify.

64| Educational Psychology

Educational Psychology focuses on how we learn and the factors that influence it . Educational Psychology influences many aspects of education, including how schools are organized, how teachers teach, how educational policy is developed and how learning materials are written, organized and/or presented in education settings. It has applicability in counseling/therapy, public education, the workplace and other sectors besides schools. Educational Psychologists tend to identify themselves as researchers and consultants, rather than as School Psychologists who work in schools.

65| Experimental Psychology

Experimental Psychology refers to the scientific means of ascertaining reasons for our thoughts, feelings, behaviors, learning and more. It may be applied to any scientifically verifiable psychology. A strict interpretation might define it as behaviorism in which observable behaviors are clearly learned as a result of rewards and punishments, although more broadly, it usually means any kind of psychology with empirical evidence.

66| Health Psychology

Health Psychology is the study of how the biological, psychological and social (bio-psycho-social) aspects of being human affect health. Practitioners of Health Psychology may work, as examples, in public or private health care, public policy, research and education settings. Students of Health Psychology learn how our attitudes, beliefs and other viewpoints, social circumstances and physiological states affect health maintenance, illness, pain management and recovery from illness or physical injury.

→

67| Neuropsychology

Neuropsychology examines the associations between brain functions and behavior. It's a science that uses positron emission tomography (PET), single photon emission computed tomography (SPECT), and functional magnetic resonance imaging (fMRI) as some of its tools. It is concerned with, as examples, the changes in brain chemistry after psychological trauma and brain states of people with certain psychiatric disorders or brain damage, and how this affects cognitive, emotional and behavioral functioning. The work of Neuropsychologists often includes assessment, treatment and consultation within health care settings.

68| Personality Psychology

Personality Psychology is the study of individual personalities. It considers the uniquely characteristic thinking, emotions and behaviors of the person. There are several concepts and theories that fall under the heading of Personality Psychology. These include humanistic, developmental and biological explanations.

69| Research Psychology

Research Psychology focuses on conducting qualitative and/or quantitative studies and writing reports and articles on results to further knowledge in the field. Although quantitative research is sometimes described as objective and qualitative research is often referred to as subjective, both are considered important in the study of Psychology and usually both are part of Psychology Research training. Courses generally include, at least, Psychology concepts, theories, research design, methods, statistics, data analysis, ethics and often some therapy coursework too. Sometimes, research is one part of a job that includes counseling/therapy, or psychotherapy, and/or administrative, consulting, testing, and/or advising. Quantitative psychological research involves an emphasis on objectively measurable research methods and empirical research design. Qualitative psychological research relies on more subjective research methods, such as the use of focus groups, case studies and surveys for data.

70| Social Psychology

Social psychology examines the effects of social interaction, including beliefs, attitudes and behaviors, on the individual. People trained in Social Psychology work in a wide variety of settings, including psychotherapy and other human services, education, business, government and more. Their work may be, as just a few examples, in assisting group or team success, community organizing, changing dysfunctional group attitudes, marketing/public relations, therapy or planning. Closely allied fields are Social Work and Sociology.

71| Adlerian Psychology: Another Kind of Psychoanalytic Psychology

Adlerian Psychology, also known as Individual Psychology, is concerned with the past and the unconscious, too. It also evolved from Freud's work. This Psychology, developed by Alfred Adler, views the individual as a unique being with a particular goal orientation expressed by his or her lifestyle. Creative ability is seen as a possible differentiating factor that interferes with relationships and relationships are viewed as a positive force. Lack of relationships, or poor ones, are viewed as responsible for social isolation and this, according to the theory, leads to neuroses. Although the person has many external pressures, a past influencing her or him, internal drives and an unconscious that all have their effects, she or he still has individual choice. Helping the person to see this and recognize choices, within a supportive relationship with the therapist, is the core of Adlerian (or Individual) Psychology practice.

72| Critiques of Freud's Psychoanalytic Psychology

There have been decades of debate about Freud's ideas since his time, from positive credit to scathing criticism. Some have said that his concepts and theories cannot be scientifically proven and so, discredit them. To those not particularly wedded to empiricism, though, this hasn't been a critical issue. His developmental theory has been criticized for it's emphases on bodily functions and instinctual drives. Freud was clearly a product of his time, though, and since then, it has been recognized by most critics that he overemphasized the importance of certain sexual and other instinctual drives as a result of the Puritanism of the time in which he lived. The degree to which he overemphasized these factors is still debated. Along with this, he has been criticized as too mechanistic in his insistence on the power of instinctual drives, thus not allowing for the individual's capacity for free choice. Freud clearly has many admirers for his identification of specific defense mechanisms; so much so that these are considered in most, if not all, beginning psychology texts. He is also respected in the field for providing the roots of later theories and therapies, whether reactive -- as in the cases of Carl Jung's and Erik Erikson's works - - or more closely allied to Freud's own theories. There isn't any denying that he provided the most influential set of theories, concepts and therapies of modern psychoanalytic psychology.

73| Jungian Psychology: A Kind of Psychoanalytic Psychology

Jungian Psychology resulted as a reaction against what Carl Jung believed were the limitations of Freud's work. Jung, a disciple of Freud's, ultimately disagreed with Freud's theories of the relationships of sexuality to neuroses and human development. Jungian Psychology is considered a Psychoanalytic Psychology, but there are many differences between it and Freud's Psychoanalytic Psychology. The most well-known of these may be: the idea of archetypes to understanding the unconscious; his postulation of both an anima (female inclination) and an animus (male inclination) within the unconscious of humans; and the idea of shadow personality characteristics that we repress and therefore cause us problems when they unexpectedly resurface in our behaviors. It is included as a Psychoanalytic Psychology primarily because of its focus on the unconscious as the pathway to understanding and treating problems that were borne of the individual's past.

74| Psychoanalytic Psychology

Broadly stated, Psychoanalytic Psychology is concerned with the individual's past as explanation for the individual's current state of mind and personality. It was developed, formalized and popularized, although not wholly originated, by Sigmund Freud in the latter 1800s and early 1900s. Since then, it has spawned both multiple variations of it and reactive theories against it. Freud's version is the one most often depicted in the popular media of the person lying on a couch and a listening, wise old man seated next to the couch, taking notes. It involves focus on the unconscious mind which can be revealed, according to Freud, through dream analysis, free association, recognition of certain intrapsychic defense mechanisms and other means. Although Freud was a psychiatrist himself, it is currently a more common practice orientation to psychologists than to psychiatrists. Some of the reasons for this may be that psychiatry has necessarily focused more on medication and adopted other forms of psychotherapy too.

75| Art Psychology

Art Psychology usually refers to art therapy, but it may instead mean the psychology of art wherein a work of art is explained in psychological terms. Art therapy is a term used to describe the creation of art for therapeutic purposes, such as healing emotional wounds, learning to problem-solve and even to decrease stress. There are Art Therapists who have degrees in that, but some other therapists use art therapy too. It's often used along with other therapy methods as well. The Psychology of Art, on the other hand, is the study of art works for what they reveal about the effects of the period, culture and other circumstances on human beings at the time.

76| Forensic Psychology

Forensic Psychology is concerned with providing expert testimony within the judicial system, but is more broadly defined as applicable to any situation involving psychology and the legal justice system. As well as providing expert witness testimony, Forensic Psychologists may provide consultation to law enforcement, help shape criminal justice policy, treat people charged with sex crimes or any number of other activities within the legal system, other government systems, prisons, hospitals, private practice or elsewhere. They are most often concerned with mental illness, or psychiatric disorders, and crime.

77| Human Factors Psychology, or Engineering Psychology

Human Factors Psychology, also know as Engineering Psychology, is concerned with the interaction of people with machines for the purposes of productivity, quality and/or efficiency. Examples are how to design an office space or equipment. Human Factors Psychology looks at how to motivate workers, retain good employees, and other concerns of the workplace, especially in industry and government. A person trained in Human Factors Psychology may also be employed by the Defense Department, NASA or in other technical capacities.

78| Organizational or Industrial Psychology

Organizational, or Industrial, Psychology studies the work environment and is used to improve work results and, sometimes, worker conditions. Many settings, including businesses, universities and non-profit organizations hire people with Organizational Psychology training for human resources, management, other administrative and consultation roles.

79| Rehabilitation Psychology

Rehabilitation Psychology centers on the study and practice of methods to help people overcome or adjust to physiological or mental injuries, maladies or disabling conditions. They focus on assisting the individual to live as fully as possible in spite of any possible limitations from those conditions. They might work with people who have psychiatric disorders, developmental disabilities, brain injuries or any number of other challenges to improve or maintain certain functions of self-care, pain management, career/vocation and interpersonal relations. They may otherwise be involved in work related to rehabilitation, such as prevention, public education and advocacy roles.

80| School Psychology

School Psychology combines knowledge of education and psychology that is then used for the support of children in schools. The success of children regarding school performance, social functioning and emotions in school is the domain of School Psychologists who may consult with people involved in the child's life, counsel children and/or parents and otherwise help to ensure an atmosphere conducive to learning. Schools generally require at least a Master's in Psychology and a teaching certificate for School Psychologist positions.

81| Sport Psychology

Sport Psychology is focused on the role of the mind in athletic performance and the application of the knowledge and skills gained from athletic performance to other aspects of life and personal growth. Of particular interest to Sport Psychologists are topics such as motivation, self-confidence and team cohesion. A strong interest in sports is required for most to succeed in this field. Jobs include working wherever sports and other athletics are practiced and in health care settings that include wellness programs. A doctorate is usually required for the very limited number of jobs working with professional sports teams. Potential work is in counseling, research, teaching, consultation and planning, but may be combined with other job responsibilities.

82| Balancing Your Life in College

Seek balance in your schedule, even though it may often be difficult to fully achieve it. You may need to cut down your work hours, take fewer courses or limit your social and other leisure activities more than you're accustomed to. You don't need to cut any of these out completely, though, and you shouldn't eliminate even your social and leisure time altogether. At least a few hours of weekly leisure and social life are necessary to regeneration, providing energy for your academic work.

83| Time Management

Write down your class times, writing assignment timeliness, study times and meeting times in your daily planner. Spread your writing assignment and study times evenly throughout your week, rather than trying to do it all in one, two or three days. If you have other obligations, such as work hours, family responsibilities and personal appointments, write those down too. Be sure to schedule yourself at least 10-minute breaks for each hour of your study and writing time. Include daily and weekly time for meals, exercise and leisure, too. Allow yourself the hours you need for sufficient sleep. Remember that overbooking yourself, cramming into the night, or neglecting your nutritional, sleep, exercise and social/recreational needs will undermine your education, as well as your health.

84| Getting The Help You'll Need

You'll need to ask for help at times while you're in college. Whether you need a resource of some sort, a referral for more specialized help, need to talk out a personal or academic issue or need something else from someone, go ahead and ask. No one will expect you to have all of the answers. Ask your instructors, other campus personnel, other students and read descriptions of what's available on your campus. You'll be in college to learn and asking questions is the first step. Become familiar with all of the available student services on your campus, as well as the various academic departments. the library, financial aid office, administrative functions and other campus resources available to you. Knowing where to find the help you need will save you a lot of frustration later on, and every student needs help now and again.

85| Health and Mental Health

Sleep, nutrition, exercise, socialization, avoidance of drugs and alcohol, and safe sex or abstinence are a part of staying healthy while you're in college. While all of this may seem obvious, the need to let go after a period of stress lands many students in trouble with their physical and emotional health. It will take a good level of responsibility on your part to maintain a healthy schedule, choose friends wisely and take care of yourself while under the pressures of college. In addition, many students have outside obligations, such as work and families that can make the stressors of college even more difficult. If you become ill, see a doctor. If you find your attitude is slipping, see a counselor. Follow their recommendations. You are a unique individual, but not so different from many other students they've seen and advised. If you feel down for a period of time, find yourself drinking or using drugs to escape, or experience a frequent need to isolate yourself from other people, get help. There's no shame in this: In fact, getting help is wisdom.

86| Learn Together

Learning together can be a powerful way to study and complete assignments. Some of your college instructors will undoubtedly use paired or group learning methods in the classroom, such as by leading class discussions and assigning certain tasks to pairs and groups. Some instructors also assign work outside of class time to pairs and groups of students. The reason they do this is that they know you and your fellow students can learn in this way. You can use this method on your own too. This doesn't mean stealing the work of others, but does mean great opportunities to learn through exchanging ideas, reciting what is to be learned, reviewing your reading and asking each other questions. There is some benefit to having to put into words what you're learning, as well as hearing others' interpretations of the material. Remember the old maxim that the teacher learns more than the student? It's true that helping another student, or even formally tutoring, also helps students who teach to learn. In a broader sense, any time that you study or work on an assignment with another person, you are also developing cooperative, team, group, communication, and perhaps even diversity, skills. If you find it difficult or frustrating, it probably means it's a great opportunity for learning those skills.

87| No Cramming Allowed

You'll hear it from instructors. You'll hear it from college counselors. You'll even hear it from some of your wiser friends. Don't cram. This means no foregoing sleep to study for a test, or to complete a reading or writing assignment. If you've planned and followed a complete, balanced and written schedule, you shouldn't feel compelled to cram. Cramming results in poor test scores, little information absorbed, sloppily written papers, poor health and take can several days of valuable time to recover your regular sleep schedule. You may hear some other students who claim they cram successfully: This just means they're taking risks with their college education. If you find that you're often running up against deadlines, see a counselor about learning some more efficient time management and study skills. You may need to adjust your schedule for better balance and prioritizing, or find better ways to keep your study within time frames. If it's a one-time or once-in-awhile issue, talk to your instructor about extending a deadline for a paper or what to focus on for an upcoming test.

88| Note-Taking

Note-taking in college classes can be a challenge at first. Master it. This is a skill that will certainly benefit you. Try using an outline format and leaving out the *ands, buts, its* and so forth. Develop a few of your own common abbreviations. Write down all points emphasized verbally by the instructor and anything the instructor writes on the board. Look at your notes later the same day, before you forget that day's class content, and complete them if they aren't clear. In time, you'll see improvement. If you need more help learning to take good notes, see a counselor and you may want to read up on skills for college. A good resource is, "Becoming a Master Student," by Dave Ellis -- a book that many successful students have used.

89| Social Life in College

Find some time to join and participate in at least one group or two on campus. Volunteer to help other students. Attend college events. Mingle with other students on and off campus. Share your thoughts and feelings with the people you meet. Ask others about themselves. College is a powerful place to learn far more than you can ever learn from only a textbook. When you go to college, it may be the first time you have contact with a diverse number of people. Even if your earlier schooling, neighborhood or church provided you with this opportunity, college will probably offer an even wider spectrum of social contacts. This is a wonderful chance to learn more about others' perspectives and the world; to strengthen your social skills, help you develop positive attitudes towards others and yourself, and understand better how to negotiate the arenas of career and social life once you're out of college. Some of the people you meet in college may also turn out to be friends, and good contacts for future jobs and other resources. Some may be people you'll have disagreements with because of your different circumstances. These can all be of benefit to you. You'll very likely meet people from various age groups, religions, socio-economic conditions, ethnicities, nationalities and a wide array of other backgrounds. Enjoy this diversity, learn from it and your present and future will be richer in many ways.

90| Studying

SQ3R stands for Survey, Question, Read, Recite and Review. Remember this and practice it. It works for most students.

1) To **survey**, look first at what you need to study.

2) Write down **questions** before and as you read the material.

3) **Read** with the intent to answer questions and pay special attention to anything emphasized.

4) To **recite** means to periodically stop reading and summarize what you've learned, whether you do that aloud, in writing or just in your head.

5) When you're done reading, **review** what you've learned. For more on this, Dr. Bob Kilik's article, "Effective Study Skills," and "The SQ3R Reading Method."

There are many other sites, books and print articles on learning good study skills too. See a few of them and adopt what works for you.

91| Use a Daily Calendar in College

Good time management is required to be successful in college. This is no less true for Psychology students than students of other disciplines. A daily planning calendar is essential to good time management and you might as well get used to using one now as you'll probably need to use one in your work-life later on, too. Buy one with large enough pages per day to write down several activities, or you can make your own pages using a word processor and put the pages into a spiral notebook.

92| Psychology Job Settings

The settings in which you plan to, and initially, use your Psychology Degree can be important to deciding your academic and career path. Although you will likely work in more than one setting during your career, where you apply your education at first can be critical to your longer term career goals; later admission for a higher degree; advancement opportunity; and even if you'll remain in the field. Job setting may also, of course, be one determinant of your pay and job satisfaction. Deciding on the general types of work settings you'd like before you begin study towards your first, or even a second or third, degree may help you to choose your educational program too. Can you picture yourself working in a school or higher education setting? Do you like or dislike the thought of working in a hospital? Does the autonomy of private practice and business acumen you'd need for private practice appeal to you or might that feel too isolated to you? Do you like the ideas of supervising others, planning, policy-making, writing, public speaking, or managing budgets and programs? In other words, would you rather work in a research, administrative or direct service environment?

93| Jobs in Psychology

The Psychology job market appears to be good through 2014, according to the Occupational Outlook Handbook for 2006-2007 (2006). Where you can find a job using your Psychology Degree depends on:

1) the degree level;

2) whether you have experience working, or perhaps volunteering, in any area of psychology;

3) whether you have a degree or experience in another area;

4) the job market where you'll live and can commute from to work; and

5) what you want to do in the field and with what population.

There are many jobs requiring a degree in Psychology. Some require an Associate's Degree, some a Bachelor's Degree, some a Master's Degree and others, a Doctorate's Degree. If you have any experience in a certain setting, performing certain work or working with a particular population, this may also be included in consideration of your qualifications for a job in the field. If you have another degree, it may be applicable towards your specific area of interest in Psychology.

You should explore the job market in the area where you want to live, or seek job projections in the work for the area in which you want to live. You may want to think about whether you would be willing to move for a specific job in the field too.

Perhaps most critically to your success in the field, you should think carefully about it is you want to do in the field; in what setting; if you want to work in direct service, consultation, teaching, community education, research, administration or some other position; and what population you hope to serve directly or indirectly.

Direct service positions can include counseling, psychotherapy, patient or client education, case management, residential case work, aide work, family assistance, assessment, intake, referral, crisis intervention and other positions, depending on your degree, experience, interests and the job market in the locale you choose. Indirect service can include many types of administrative positions; research; research assistance; teaching within or for an organization, agency or higher education setting; grass roots or more formal political organizing; and other indirect service positions.

94| Jobs in Research Psychology

Consider private and public organizations, such as government departments responsible for meeting human needs, hospitals, large human service agencies and policy-making entities to discover the kinds of positions that exist in Research Psychology. Also check with a professional career counselor for this information. Professors who teach Research Psychology are a good source of this information too.

95| The Job Market

You can talk to a career counselor at a college or another location, look up information on the Internet or check in a library. One place to look is in the Occupational Outlook Handbook. This is considered an essential resource for job market projections. If you look at the Handbook or elsewhere, you can use the keywords; psychology, social work, human services, psychotherapists, counselors and other related occupations. Many of those are listed in the Handbook under, "Related Occupations" (2006). The Handbook can also tell you what generally required qualifications you would need. If using the Internet, you can pair your keywords with other keywords too, such as; careers, career projections, job market projections and so forth. The Handbook also lists projections by state. In addition, you can see your state's Dept. of Labor, Employment Security and Workforce web sites for job market projections. They aren't listed on all state's web sites, but you'll find the projections for most states. Many colleges and universities list job market projections on their web sites too.

96| Psychology Degrees for Counseling and Therapy

Most therapy and counseling positions require a Master's Degree in Psychology or a related field, such as Social Work. They usually don't distinguish between a Master's in Arts or Master's in Science. Before you decide, though, you should be sure to check with a few places where you can see yourself working to ask what the qualifications are for the kind of work you want to do. Ask for the human resources department or a person responsible for hiring therapists or counselors. You may also find some relevant information from people you know who work in the field and from certain psychology career web sites pertaining to the location in which you hope to be employed. Once you have solid information written down, look at the range of qualifications. What are the qualifications in common between the sites you contacted? Did you contact at least four or five employment sources? Don't limit your investigation to less and try not to hear only what you want to hear. Apply some objectivity to the task. Later, you can combine this information with your more subjective inclinations. At first, though, you need to get the facts so that you don't go too far down an unrealistic or uninformed path.

97| Job Opportunities with a Doctorate in Psychology

Private psychology practitioners can be licensed as Psychologists with a Doctorate in Psychology. This allows the professional to work in private psychology practice. Some states require a passing score on a test, a fee for the license and proof of the degree. Doctoral level psychologists are also frequently employed in schools, government programs, hospitals and other health care, in disability settings and other education, justice, human service and health care organizations. They may work as counselors, psychotherapists, college-level instructors, researchers, consultants, trainers and several other capacities. They are often called on to supervise other employees, serve on committees, direct programs, conduct research, perform psychological assessments, serve as expert witnesses, write reports and academic articles and do other administrative and highly responsible therapy, counseling and training work. For more information, you can ask professors who teach doctoral level Psychology courses and a career counselor knowledgeable in doctoral level psychology who may be based at a college or university; survey the job market in your intended locale; see the employment and recruitment ads; and check certain education and career web sites.

98| Service Populations

Think about the populations you would like to serve as you consider possible job settings. You may be interested in serving seniors and elderly people, children, people with disabilities, adolescents, people of a certain ethnic or religious background, couples, employees, job-seekers, families, people with mental illnesses (or psychiatric disorders), immigrants, probationers, prisoners, or other people with certain specific issues, goals or challenges. There is a very wide range of possibility. Thinking about the issues you are interested in can help you decide what population you want to work with too. Some of the issues of people who are served by paraprofessionals and professionals are; drug abuse and addiction, infertility, adoption issues, disability challenges, death and dying, academic issues, childhood abuse issues, anger and aggression and many others. Whether you choose to work with people who have mental illnesses, also called psychiatric disorders; people who have life issues, but not necessarily serious psychiatric diagnoses; or people who are seeking help with self-improvement, there are many different challenges they face. You may be able to help them with these if you have a Psychology Degree with the training appropriate to those issue(s).

99| Working with a Psychology Associate's Degree

There are human service jobs where you can use an Associate's Degree in Psychology, depending on the job market where you will live and hope to work. Some of these might be; teacher's aide, case management aide, family support aide, residential case manager, government benefits case worker, teen mentor, childcare worker and other possibilities. These are usually entry-level positions, although with experience there might be opportunity to advance in some organizations. This will depend on the organization and the work. Some people with Associate's Degrees work in resource referral positions, in human resources, in development (fund raising and grant writing, as examples) and in grass roots campaigning, political action and organizing capacities. Some people with Associate's Degrees work in hospital, human services and education reception and admissions positions. They may also work as testing assistants, training assistants, psychiatric hospital technicians and in any number of other capacities where psychology can be put to practical use. Again, check with a college-based or other career counselor, do your own job market survey, as described under, "Degrees for Counseling and Therapy," and look at job market projections for health, education and human services sectors. You may want and need to work in one of these jobs while you continue your education towards another degree, perhaps a Bachelor's, a Master's and even a Doctorate in Psychology. Many professionals start out with an Associate's Degree in Psychology.

100| Working With a Psychology Master's Degree

The Master's Degree in Psychology, or Social Work, is often considered the backbone of human services and is necessary for school counseling, community college teaching, college student counseling and many other responsible, interesting, professional and middle income earning positions. you may also be eligible, with your Master's, for private practice as a therapist or counselor, depending on licensing certification and perhaps, registration laws in your state. However, you probably cannot be licensed as a Psychologist without a Doctorate in Psychology. You can ask instructors who teach Master's level Psychology courses and a career counselor; survey the job market in your intended locale; see the employment ads; and check certain education and career web sites for more, and local, job market information. Although a Master's in Psychology is usually a very marketable degree, job markets vary from area to area.

More Titles in the LifeTips Book Series

101 Student Loan Tips
by Jennifer Mathes

101 Health Insurance Tips
by Michelle Katz

101 Autism Tips
by Tammi Reynolds

101 Substance Abuse Recovery Tips
by Blythe Landry

Printed in the United States
132067LV00004B/8/A

9 781602 750128